Endangered Animals

Of the World

Big Print
Colouring Book

This book belongs to:

____

The Giant Koala
From China

The Orca
From United States

The Puffin
From Iceland

Galápagos Penguin
From the Galápagos

Chinese Water Deer
From China and Korea

The Siamese Crocodile
From Asia

The Siberian Tiger
From Russia

The Fossa
From Madagascar

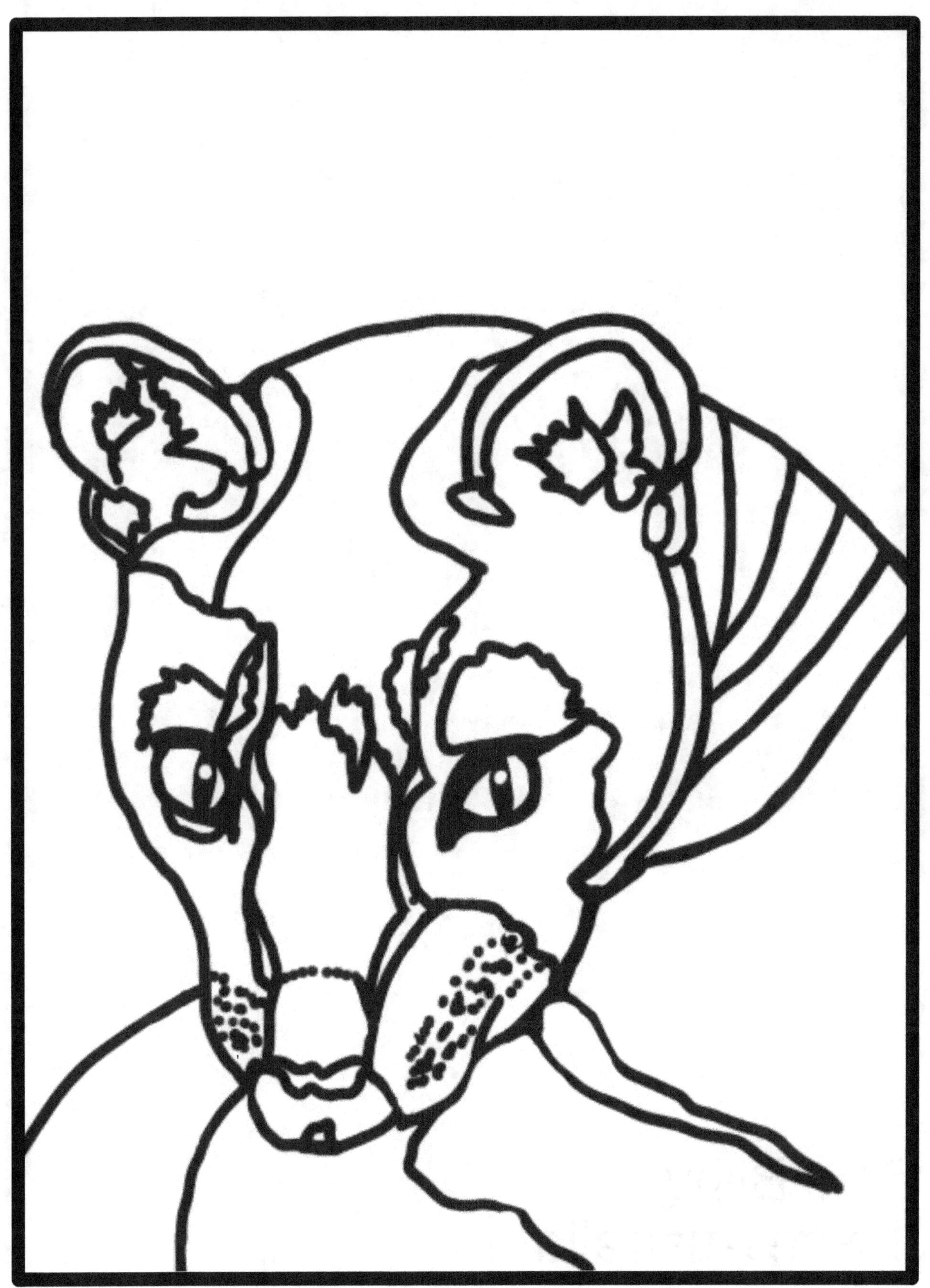

The Bilby
From Australia

The Wombat
From Tasmania

The Giraffe
From Africa

The Coatimundi
From Mexico & United States

Green turtle
From Atlantic, Indian,
& Pacific Ocean

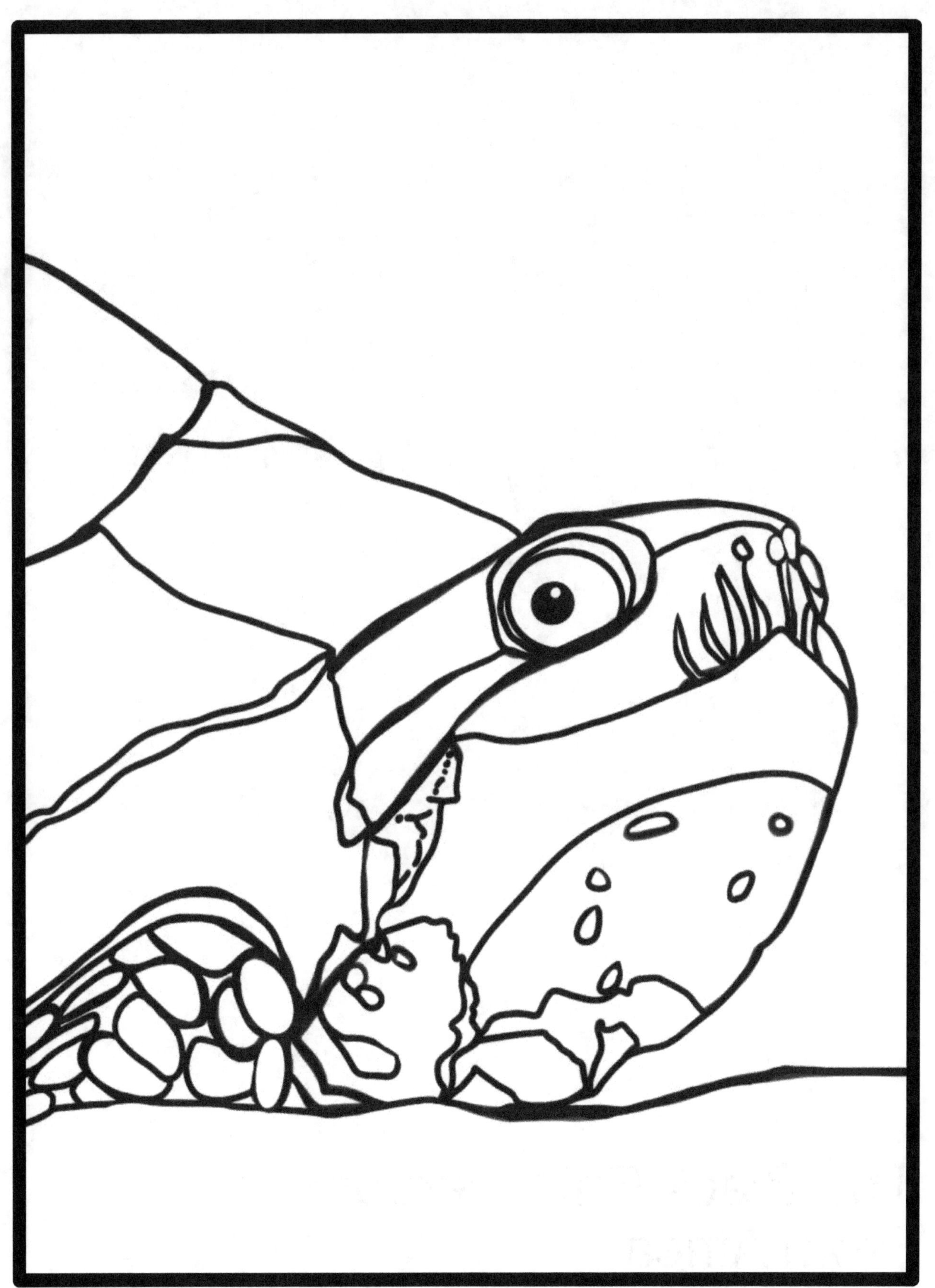

The Black Rhinocerous
From Africa

The Umbonia Spinosa

From South America

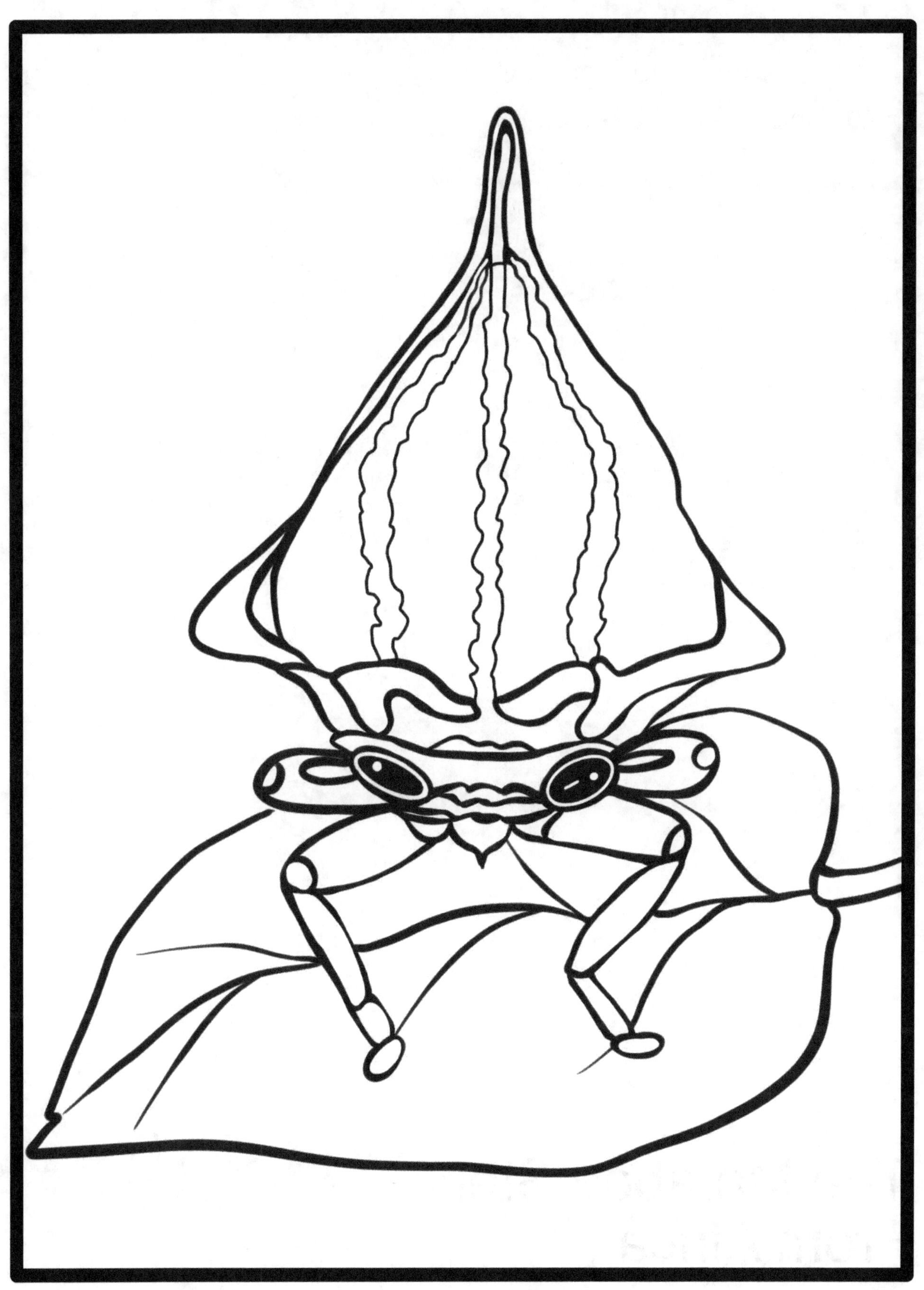

The Marabou Stork
From Africa

The Dik Dik
From Africa

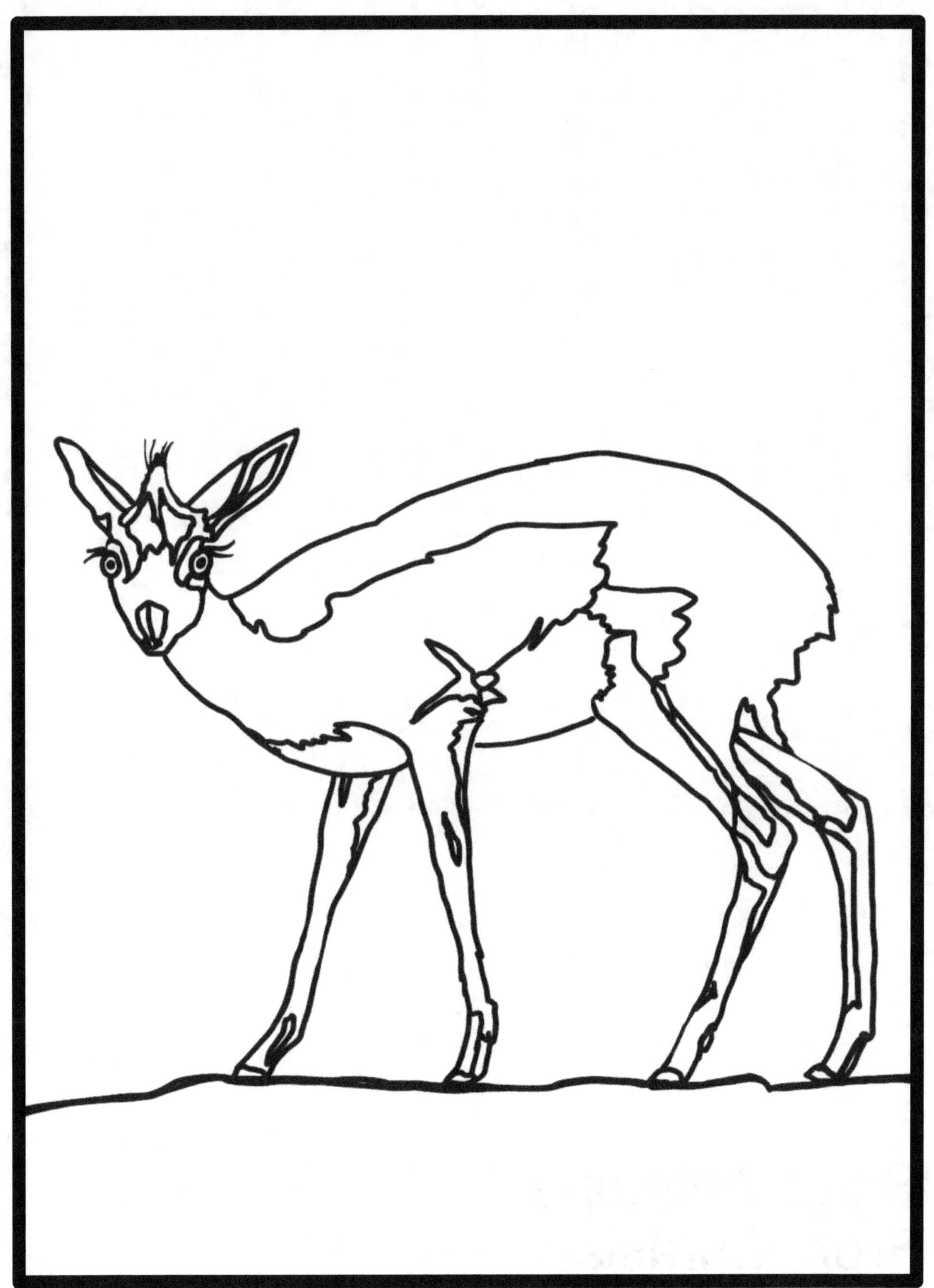

Saiga Antelope
From Eurasia

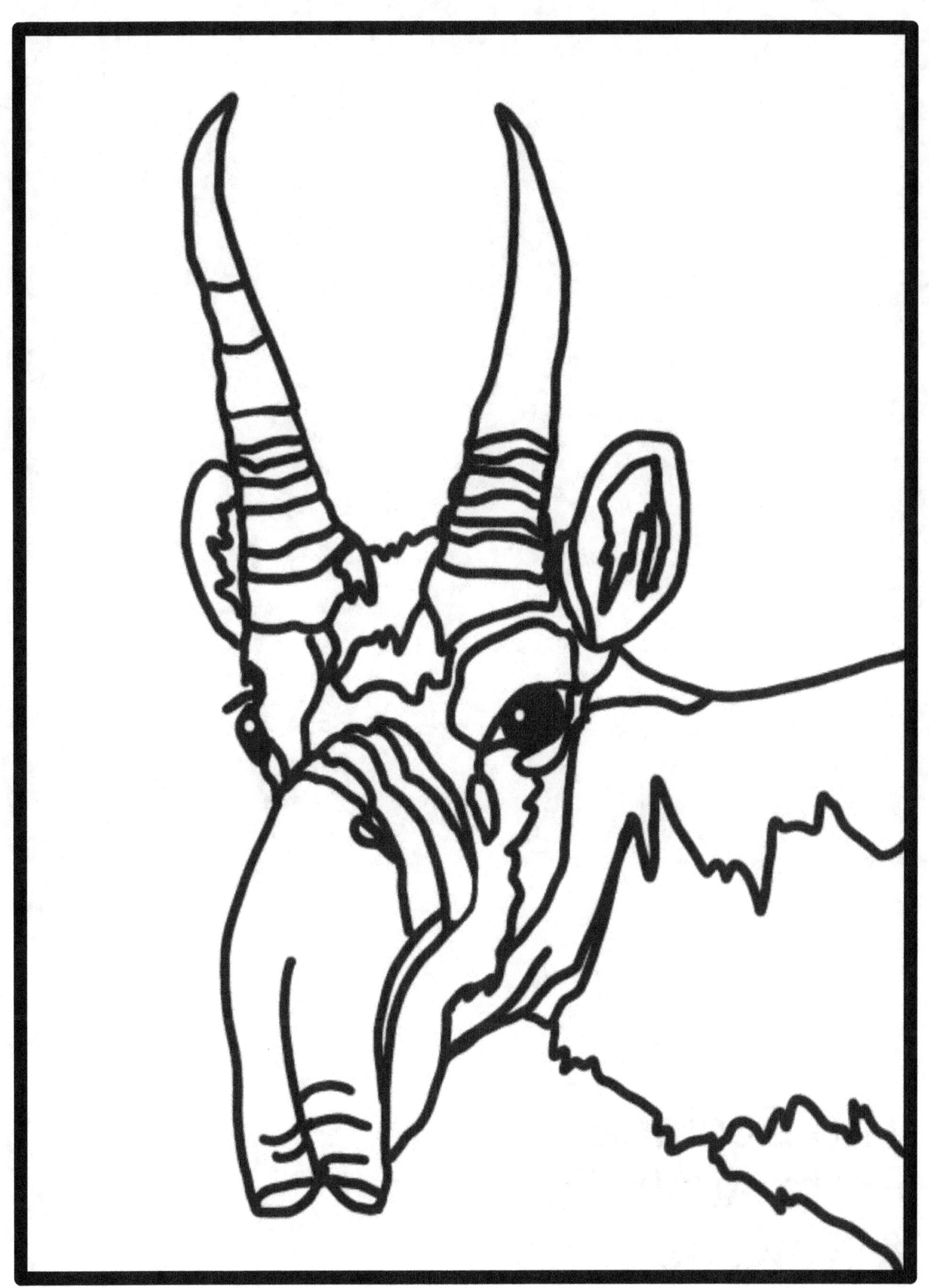

The Echidna
From Australia
& New Guinea

The Jerboa
From Asia, North Africa

The Duck-billed Platypus
From South Australia
&Tasmania

The Peacock Spider
From Australia

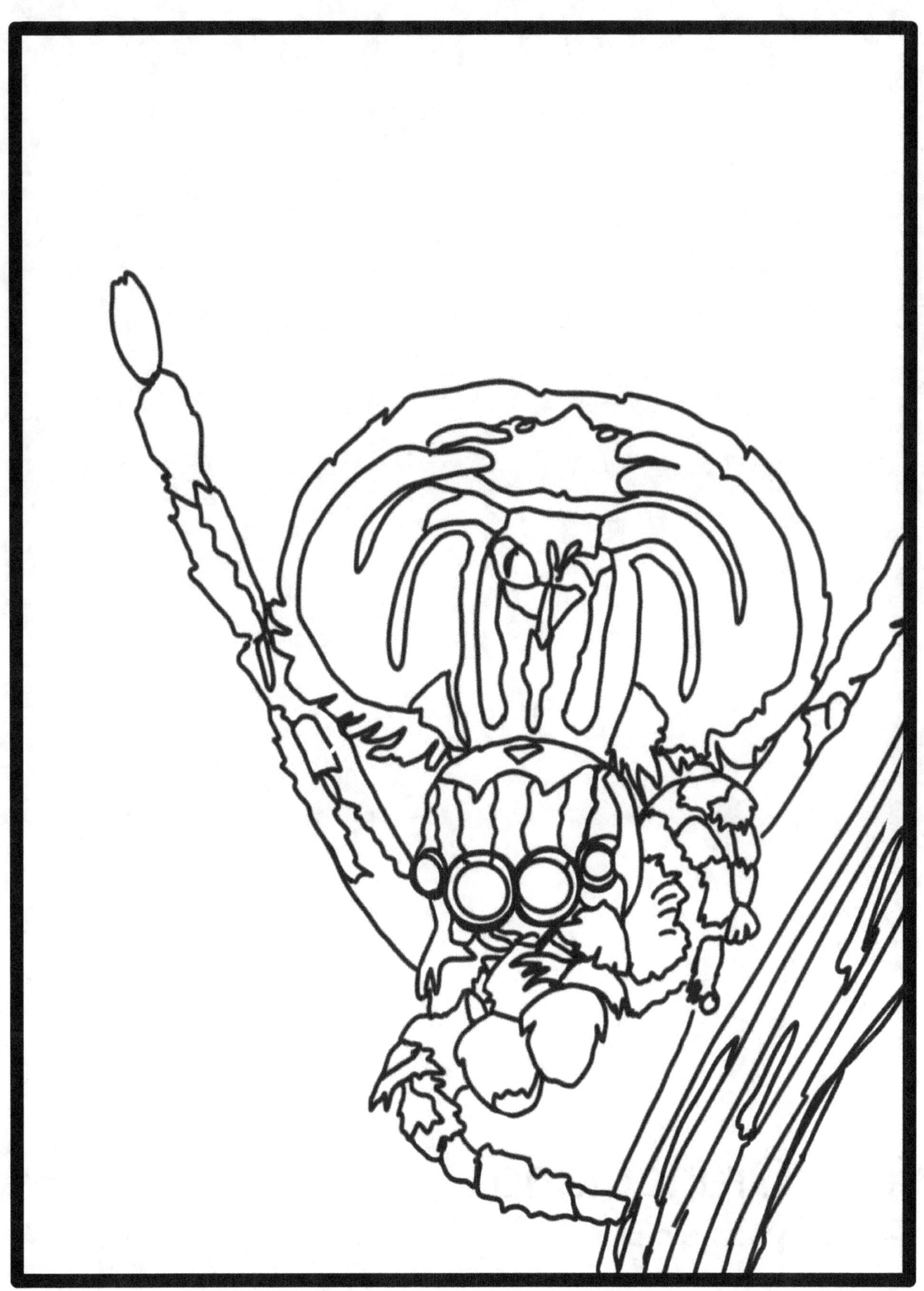

The Orangutang
From Africa

The Vaquita

From the Gulf of California

The Leopard,
From China

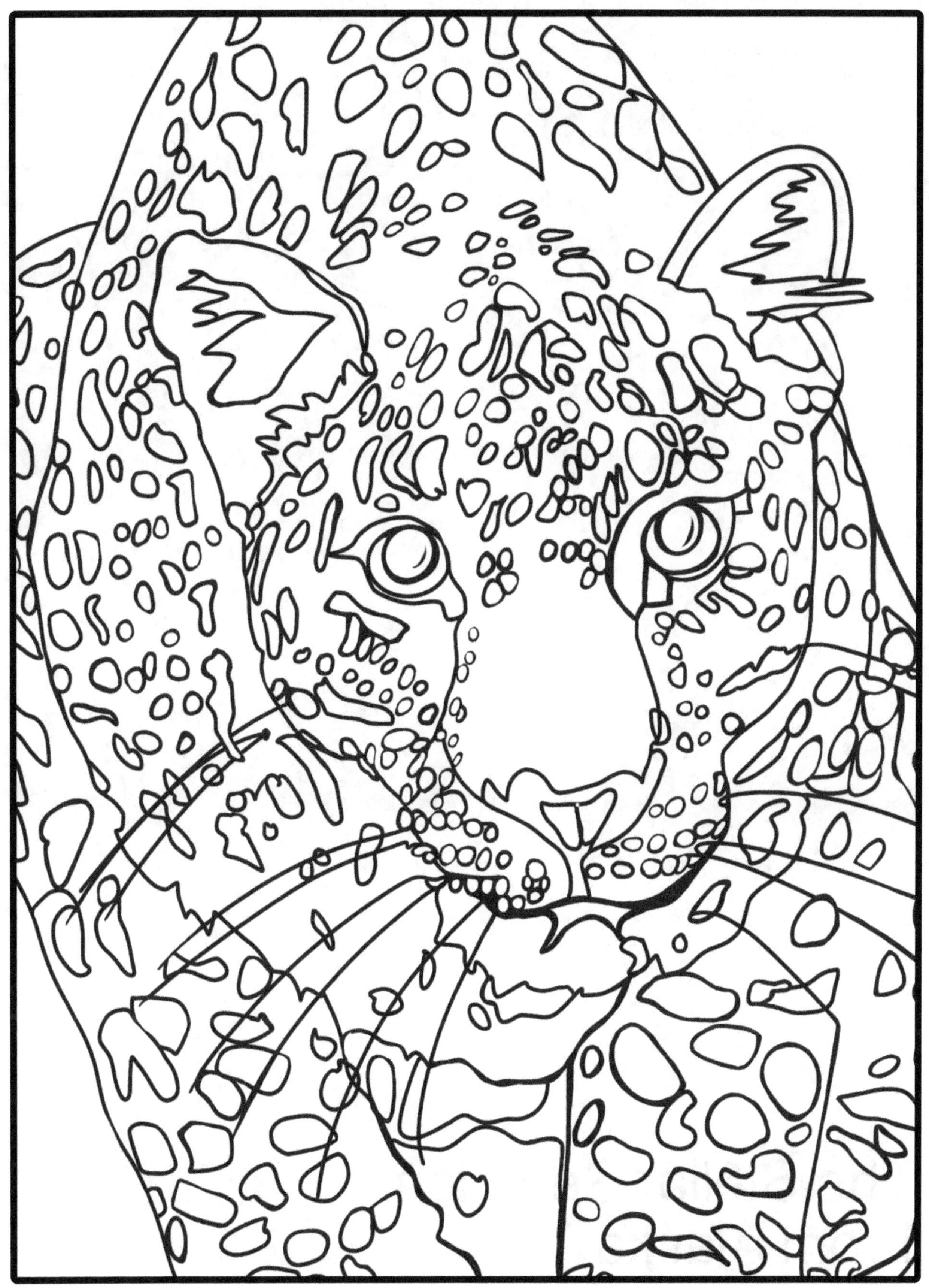

The Stellar Sea Lion
From Alaska

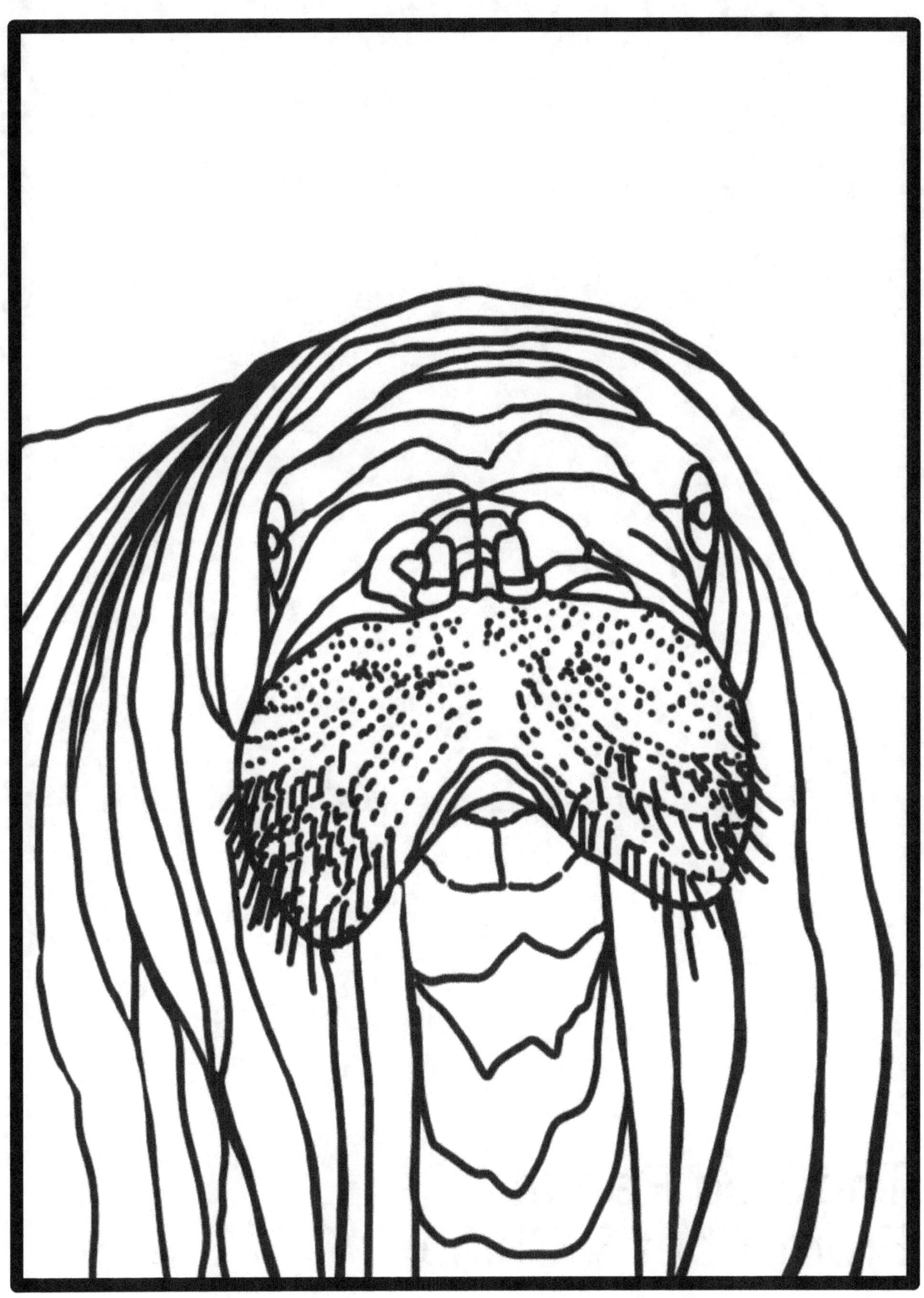

The Red Panda
From Tibet & China

TheYellow Seahorse
From Dorset, United Kingdom

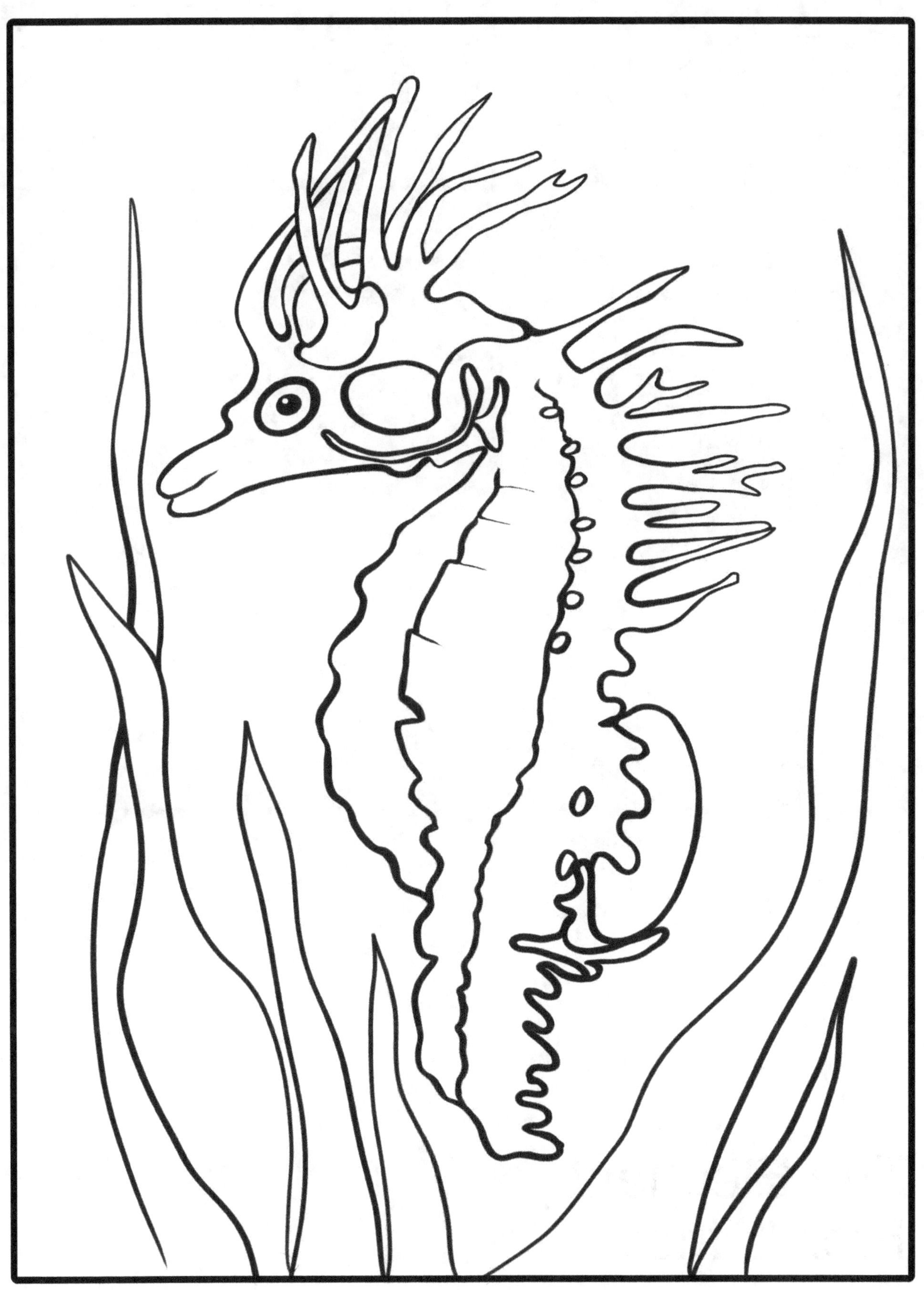

The Elephant
From Africa

The Lowland Gorilla
From Africa

Look for my next Colouring
Book - Endangered Animals
Of North America